C000263336

crossing paths

crossing paths

by
-f.a.peeke-

First published 2018 in the United Kingdom by Vurse1 Publishing

Contact: vurse1publishing@gmail.com

Text © 2018 f.a.peeke

Photography © 2018 f.a.peeke

The right of f.a.peeke (Fiona Peeke) to be identified as the author of this work has been asserted by her in accordance with the Copyright, Designs and Patents Act 1988.

All rights reserved. No part of this publication (words or photographs) may be reproduced, stored or introduced into a retrieval system, or transmitted, in any form or by any means without the prior written permission of the publisher and copyright owner, except in the case of reprints in the context of reviews.

ISBN 978-1-9999315-0-6

Visit: www.fapeeke.com

Photo Edits by Scott Wackett

crossing paths

From me to you:

When I was seven years old I wrote my first set of lyrics and put them to the tune of 'Oranges and Lemons'. It was inspired by a strange fascination I'd adopted for two majestic Afghan Hounds called, Simba and Suki. They lived across the street from us and I was mesmerised every time I saw them. The song was, in essence, hideous – but none the less I sang it over and over again for about three weeks; driving my father almost insane. In view of the fact he'd been the very person to tell me to 'write it down' if ever I felt I couldn't say something out loud, the poor man really had no option but to put up with my words, whatever form they arrived in.

It remains, to this day, one of the few memories I can recall from this period in my childhood and still makes me smile to think that from one terrible song and a father's good advice, sprang a life-long passion for poetry and rhythm.

About the book:

The poetry in this collection covers a montage of subjects, situations and emotions that, I feel, are not exclusive to any age, sex or religion. As a human being, not just as a woman, I have been on first name terms with some of the most abhorrent feelings I hope never to come face to face with again. But I have learnt that discrimination, heartache, grief, joy and love are universal and they are certainly not biased. They come in many forms and affect us all, without exception, regardless of who you are or what you have.

It was from this sobering realization that *crossing paths* was initially conceived and has been written with a sense of travelling in mind.

The many different paths that present themselves to us during our travels can lead towards friendship, love and desire, whilst others take us towards loss, anger and pain. More often than not, these journeys run a parallel race – weaving unique and unusual aspects of the course together, making us question solid fact and feel things we never thought possible.

For me, crossing these paths is an inevitable part of the adventure if we are to keep learning and growing; if we are to become the people that those who look most affectionately upon us, already see.

Personal note on book:

I write words in the hope that they will be read aloud. There is a sway and a tempo to each piece that I believe becomes more apparent when read in this way. My wish is only that you allow the words to rumble and vibrate through you until they find a comfortable (or uncomfortable) place to rest. For me, it is a fine feeling indeed to form my own melodies, sounds and rhythms and provide a beat that leads the way and takes me with it on its journey.

The dated pieces throughout the book are diary excerpts. Free flowing thoughts, ideas and emotions that usually arrive in the dead of night.

It felt only natural to include a few of my own photographs in this collection, as I see them as extensions of my thoughts and feelings.

There is no table of contents in *crossing paths*. There is no formula to follow as, like life, sometimes the most eventful paths are the ones you walk without planning. I wish you love and understanding on your journey.

-f.a.peeke-

For all of those
who wear their heart on their sleeve,
but keep a little bit of crazy in their pocket.

15th February 2016 - 2.05am

It took me a long time
to feel happy with myself
    inside
        outside
blindsided by expectations
      and opinions
that roamed like aliens
      around my heart
playing bigger parts in my movie
      than me.
I read from transient scripts
whilst I waited for something
monumental to happen
    life changing
        mind blowing
something to define a purpose
- owning a reason to exist -
instead of walking out on stage
   letting go of the need
to persist with the insanity
      and be content
          to just play me.

This Thing We Call Living

Don't you want to see it coming
Head on
Straight at you
Knowing it's going to burn
But standing firm anyway
Just so you can feel it?

Don't you want to be
In the driving seat
Picking out your own cd
Singing to the one
With the tunes of your life
Torn through it?

Don't you want to fill yourself
Up with it?
Stand underneath your own decisions
- Right or wrong -
And let them soak you.
Purify your soul.

Don't you want to take a step back
Absorb the whole goddam
Mess of it all?
Smile and cherish the call
Of this world
The one you created for yourself.

Don't you want it all?

4th January 2016 - 11.56pm

What does being one's
truest self mean?
I am a different *self*
on different days.
These many faces I wear
so comfortably
are all a part of my
- truest self -
just with different
pleasantries.

The Kindness Around Us

I love to see the
    Richness in the sky
Reflect onto the earth's
    Soft, green flesh
Watch it mesh together
And move as one tribe
                - One family -
Sweeping the land
    Hand in hand it rolls
Measuring time and love
     Counting the strength
That finds a home within it.

First Dance

Instructing the darkness to excite
The lights dimmed
All but one
 A broken lamp
Blinking intermittently
  Winking flippantly
In honour of the night.
The air -
 Musty
  Thick
The music -
 Old
  Memorable.

It made me smile
To breathe in the cinnamon
Of my childhood.
No good in trying to stop.
 I swayed
Allowing the sound
To take me
 Eyes closed
It embraced me
And when they opened
I held my breath
 Chest beating out
The rhythm of you.

Your amber body
Moved closer
My composure
Begged its leave
And as you held out
Your hand
 My heart knew.

You slipped an arm
Around my waist
      I could taste
Salt on my lips
And the harsh kick of
Whisky in my throat.
Denim touched denim
And as you pulled me in
My cheek found its place
      Next to your chin.

We were transformed.
Rough blue turned to finest
      Silk and satin
Battling a desire as old
      As time.
Sassy dripped from
The speakers
And the lamp glistened with
      A thousand
            Teardrop crystals.

You whispered when you
Asked me my name
Like it was our game
And no-one else was invited.
I replied with a kiss
      Bliss seeping
Through my bones
And you responded
With a dance
That has lasted
      A lifetime.

Silent Cowardice

I want you to see inside
  - Open me up -
And find
The shades I'm too
Ashamed to paint
     My outside with.
Let your touch
Slice through bone
And know that when you're done
What's exposed
Is everything my body
     Longed to give.
Dissect my past mistakes
The one's that I daren't speak of
   For fear of
Losing any chance
   To make
     You stay.
Carve through this shell
Called me
And find the part of this machine
That's swallowed
     Screams of bravery
And keeps my young heart scared.

15th September 2016 - 4.10am

Us fools follow a different path
where weeds and nettles thrive
        - erupting sweetly -
                together they dance
with no-one to rip them
        from the earth
                and call them ugly.

A Question for Your Thoughts

Did you ever want them to call you beautiful?
Not a name I would choose as my title.

Your flaws left transparent and whispering
Like they had no secrets of their own
        And nervously listening to the spite
                That spreads and spews
Over the covers of your world
            Then hand-rolled and delivered
            Back to you
            - Presented and served by silver-tongued
      mules -
Who offer their elaborate explanations
Bound by ribbons laced with promises and rules.

            I want none of it!
Their beauty is not mine to want or need.
The seed of their truth grows in different lands
My beauty stands in acceptance and surrender
Independence remembered and given back to my heart.
        So I ask…
                Where is your beauty?
                Where does it live?
                Does it hide in the mirror?
Or is it someplace you can't forgive them
                For not finding?

31st December 2016 - 3.15am

When you are stripped
of everything you have:
   your love
      your strength
   your sense of self
      - your peace -
instead of lifting your face
     towards the sky
        for answers
            you've been denied
look at the image your parents made.
    Be grateful.
Take your scared and timid finger
and touch the rawness
- the beating mess within your chest -
    feel it
       taste it
and know
    perhaps for the first time
that this is your gift
    to yourself:

          an open heart.

Pale Memory

- I remember -
Words spoken softly
Kindness sprinkled
On every syllable
Smiling eyes
Wore their unforgettable
Happiness as I watched
Them dress to greet me
- Love me -
Beat me at my own game.
Your tone of heart
Sparked moments fuelled by
A lifetime of silent pain.
- I remember -

Thank You

Your smile,
   A calm sea
      In the storm,
       Remains a
Constant grace.
    Removing tears
     That used
To drown
   The skin
     Upon my face.

Battleground

Fight your battles somewhere else.
        Leave our babies unharmed
Amongst the rubble
            Of your degeneration.
        Elimination is not
On our agenda
  - Their blood is our blood -
            Red and thick and pure
            It flows strong
        Along with the unrest.

Can you feel it?

        Were you there when
            Your disease
            Spilled into our streets?
The cure was a test
        You set for us
            With no clues to help.
All you've given us is fear
        To build on
            Smeared over us
                It clings on
            Like a rumour
                Infecting
                    Inciting
        Rejecting chances to begin again
                Without you.

Fight your battles somewhere else
Your guns aren't welcome here.
          The tears still flow
                    From before.
          Cries echo in homes
                    That have long since
          Been reduced
                    To two walls.

Call your friends
          Tell them
                    No more
Our babies cannot
          Settle your scores.

9th November 2016 - 11.25pm

On the day the world went crazy
some sanity returned to mine.

The ambition of the reprobate
shone through the crowds of the confused

- and won nothing but a scared nation -
waiting to see whether the wall was real

and who would build it.
Waiting to realise who it was

that needed protecting.
Us or them?

1st March 2017 - 1.55am

I couldn't tell
at first
exactly what it was
that had changed
until I blamed you
and realised
it was me.

27th January 2017 - 12.50am

Do I really need to be reminded
of your past again?
After all these years
would you not rather talk about
the past we have in common?
The one we have made together
grown amongst the tangled
weeds of 'before'.
Let's pluck its ripe, fresh fruit
from our memories
and taste its gentle sweetness
as we recall the day we met.
Or would you prefer to pick at
the bitter pulp that stings
our lips with its sourness
and pricks our soft palates
with its thorns?

Ms Waymon Goddam

She was an eruption surging.
   A split forming
         In the earth's crust.
   A wave building
Thrusting its way
    Over rocks and stars
Drenching them.
   Fulfilling them.
She was a deep chasm
     Fathomless
Mesmerising and intriguing
     Torn in two
Bleeding for her peoples fight.
    No rights
But still she rose.
She was a fire that a million
Hands tried to hold
    Charmed by its glow
Expecting the flame to absolve
Them of their ignorance.
She was more than a voice
Although she sang like a soul
That had been scorched
    A thousand times.
Branded by a stigma that was
    Unfamiliar
Hoping her desire would become
    Insular
        But it never would.

Not even in her haze
		- Days upon days of mist -
		She could not breathe through
Her passion still clung to her
Like a starving child at a breast.
Insatiable and needy
		Greedy and desperate for more.

Her body quickly lived
		Cursed with a gift
		That lifted revolutions then watched her demise.
As the world stumbled and choked
		On spoon-fed lies
The High Priestess laid down her gauntlet
		But never realised her true sound
		The one her soul had drawn
Pictures of in her mind.
			The portrait she deserved
			To paint and leave behind.

I Left the Flowers

I left the flowers there
Alone on a shaded summers day
Where no-one dared to look
- My heart foolishly mistook -
            Their sincerity
                    For atrocity
Instead of dulling
            Animosity
They fuelled the disillusionment
That lay deep within
            My weakened mind.

I wanted you to see
But ripened feelings had diluted
            Drowned in waters deep
                With no trace of a struggle
I couldn't keep
            Us afloat
                    Alone.
Your raft wasn't big enough
            For two.
Arrogance watched me set sail
            For new lands.
            New adventures.

Worship the Silence

Trying to find what lies within it
What makes me feel I have to
Fill it with words and gestures
Unable to support me?
Wasted sounds spew out and
Astound uncomfortable listeners
Who politely nod my
Embarrassment away
And pretend it's ok
– but it's not.

When did this need become a habit?
An involuntary addiction
When did the silence speak
And tell me it was lonely?
  Slowly prompting me
      Closely following me
Until I joined it in its premonition
Of chagrined agony.
But it seems the woe is mine
- When time is absorbed by me -
          Or my words.

Fractions splinter away and tiny pieces
Of the whole can be left
Without being filled
Bereft of noise and polluted views.
          Gaps appear
Clues, pointers, directing you
To the honest place inside
That asks:
What is there to be afraid of
In that hole

That world of nothingness?
Barely seen by the confident and strong
I long for the blindness
That afflicts them
I pray for the courage
That assists them
     In that moment
When they allow themselves
                    To stop.

To block emotion from the scene
Enjoy the lack of chaos
Let my breath, not commotion,
- Reign supreme -
Suck in the air around my cheeks
And blow out careless weeks
Without a thought of who I may offend.
But, it seems, the silence brings
Old friends to visit
And warms its hands
To clasp around my throat
And choke me
Until despair eventually
Soaks me with its approval.
     And there it is
The beauty in the air around me
The pause in the race
The wondrous space
Is filled
And thick with irrelevance again.
Next time, I say, next time
The words will
Stay inside.
Next time, I say, next time
A lullaby will hold them in
Sweet slumber.

Next time.

22nd October 2016 - 1.19am

We stopped each other
from being alone
by ignoring the exhausting
swathe of emptiness
that had wrapped itself
around our hearts
    squeezing gently and relentlessly.
- We reached for each other -
   and as our hands touched
      solitude rose
         and made its excuses.

17th August 2016 - 1.22am

Electricity pierced my throat
and all hope left
- along with my breath -
   the first time you touched me.
         My skin felt as though
   it had been
         ripped
               scorched
                     loved like fire
            and desire found me full.

Transition

Moving between worlds
- You touched my tears -
Before you left.
Your warm breath
Shone last moments
Of love
Over the lonely
Ice-tipped mountains
That my grief sat upon.
Just for a second
Your glow lit the moon
And it consumed us completely
As we grew whole again.
    As we went home again.

Free to Fall

I felt like a leaf
Ripped from its birthplace
By the autumn breeze
Flying towards fields ablaze
With orange, red and green
Endeavouring to make my
Descent count for something
- Spectacular and unique -
I was exquisitely alone
In my attempt to be profound
And the sound of me falling
Echoed harmonies of sweet
        Nothings
Until I exhaled my last
Gratifying breath
And made my peace
        With the ground.

Bridges

It wasn't far away
The distance between
'Hello' and 'I love you!'
Certainty pulled us
From the comfort of my
Mother's juniper cologne.
Alone, we came together
Never thinking of the
Seconds to come.
Undone by each other's
   Voice
      Touch
         Breath.
We walked from one
Side to the other
- Breaking oaths -
Betrothed by fate.
Our bridge took us
On a journey
That would lose us
      Forever.

Boxing Day

Ripping through me
With family ties

Pulling tighter

The one's that choke and suffocate the lies
The one's that say we were once close
When most people know that's not true.

Is it me or you
Or both of us
That doesn't care?

When age allows
The final breath to share
Its honesty with my heart
I'll know we were apart
For a reason.

No Man's Land (an Amazonian Dilemma)

What is this place?
Where unspoken catastrophes
Sit down to eat with the masters of extortion
And where consequences cannot resurrect us
From a global emptiness that ages forged with blood
Trodden down
Underground
Where the weak and the scared are easily re-cycled
As the strong and the heartless
Rule a conscience-free world.

Who can understand?
They stare, mesmerised, confused
Ostracized by an unforgiving world
That tells them they know best
- Watching outsiders -
With painted egos marching on
Disrupting peace when war has gone
To feed an endless greed
And drain the life
From a diminished culture.

Where is the love that favoured men
And their elaborate speeches?
Transforming night to day
Only to wash away
The glorious stain that hope leaves
On a diluted dream of forgotten souls
Dragging their hearts out to the street
For all to witness their surrender
And celebrate in their defeat.

When can they stop?
A nomadic life that was not chosen
Whimpering at the heels of a society
That turned its back
As dealers shook hands
With disregard, contempt and lies
Filling their stomachs and their purses
Watching their bank balance thrive
And leaving scraps in no man's land
Where no man can survive.

Look to See

Not seeing for an age, as a child would
Every day this sight passes blinded eyes.

The contrasting colours moving
Swaying, stroking the blue sky.

Titian arms reaching out
Offering the chance of a fusion

Perfect, unattainable and at peace
With their disparity.

Gliding gracefully in each other's space
With no air of discomfort.

They have welcomed one and other home
And cleared a path to my heart.

21st May 2017 - 12.21am

I've been numb since
I was nineteen.
My whole life
has rolled from one
unimaginable scene
to another
- movies that Mr King -
would revel in
and moments that
I would gladly forget
if my mind would
allow me to remember.

Last Night

You spoke to me last night.
What did you say? I can't remember.
Your face looked drunk with pain
Your coal black eyes dug into mine
So deeply that I dare not keep a secret.

I felt you by my side
But never really there at all
A distant place – a Neverland
Holds your passion far away from me.
And I cannot compete.

It feels like déjà vu to see you
One that meant so much to me
I can't remember hours or days
Or how you loved me.
Was it deeply?

You spoke to me last night.
What did you say? I know it's important.
The touch that I had longed for
Sadly never came
Although your tone clung to me for days.

Did you come to tell me the world awaits?
Breathing undertones of truth
In hope-filled pools.
The words of the wise are drowning still
With ears that hear less than my eyes.

And I cannot recall
A time when others too could touch you.
Faded by a life of guilt and blame
That can't remember minutes or seconds
Or last words spoken.
Feint broken fragments remain my only friend.

2nd January 2017 - 10.50pm

The silence
  is only lonely
when the space
      is filled
          with regret.

30th March 2017 - 10.35pm

I watch her
    as she's talked at.
Her eyes drifting
shifting into thoughts of
- what she longs to say -
what she wants to scream.
The world around her
slides out from its
ever-changing reality
as morality opens its mouth
to speak to a culture
    that stands by
and watches her hurl
        her voice into
the blistering heat
    whilst it happily
        looks away.

Hidden

What is she to you?
'A dirty face – her race
They're all the same.'
Her shame?
Hidden well.
Is it under her veil?
If it's not, what is?
'Ms, I can't see under there
And if I can't see
Then there's something to hide
   - Inside, not out.'
But we all hide.
What makes her secret
Worse than yours?
       Dangerous.
Her cause is not what you think -
But still you drink it up
And quench the thirst of your nation
Until salvation is a foreign promise
That doesn't apply here.
Whether she lives next door
Or worlds away
You'll say:
'As long as she doesn't
Come near me.
Lock her out, all her kind'
     Never mind that
She has no home
Or shown compassion
At your disgrace
We'll make her face the firing squad
'Line up, line up
It's time to meet your God!'

The hate that hates another
Will run blindly
Searching
For comfort and cover
When the time comes to explain.
She weeps for your confusion
           And your fear
Her tears are for your soul, not hers.
She hears a different song from yours
One that sees all
           Wrongs put right
A place where hatred
           Absconds
And hearts mend without a fight.
That's what she keeps
Inside, not out
Her melody of hope
     When days of darkness cast their doubt.

Guilty Sons

It didn't cross his mind
- When fatal eyes sunk in sorrow -
That never again would light welcome him
In his fumes of pity and self-harm.
He wallowed safely
Without fear or knowledge
Allowing shadows of consequence to call his name.

Help was always near to pierce his skin
But too far away to dress the wounds.
Shallow bridges long since burnt
With the embers of memory fading, like her breath.
She rested hopelessly
- While it didn't cross his mind -
And listened for the sound of his song.

Struggling daily in her solitude
Praise and relief are a mother's affliction
But no such pardon seemed granted here
In a womb made from duty and promises.
And all the time
- It didn't cross his mind -
To open his silent heart and talk to hers.

15th February 2017 - 2.12am

I am happy to hold hands with you
happy to shed tears with you
happy to stare into the nothing with you
happy to wait for the birds to sing again with you
happy to listen to the crack your heart makes with you.
I am happy to be sad with you
    - my love -
        my friend.

5th June 2016 - 9.25pm

I'm a little rough around the edges.
I'm not what you'd call
sweet or twee or
afraid to say what I mean.
I don't fart rainbows
I have thunder inside.
I don't speak when I'm told to
and sip expensive fine wines
I swear and drink whisky
and simplicity is my best friend.
I'm sorry, I don't know
how to be any other way.
You tell me I'm strange
but it's ok
I don't mind that.
I don't mind you.
Please,
don't mind me.

The Source

It springs from the soul of the earth
Life inspired
By a simple existence
High above the mist of evolution
Where God and the mountains
Converse.

A nameless agenda is clear
Indefinable
And restless in its course
Arousing the constant flow
- It quickens -
Drenching the land with
Luminous tears.

Softly the wounded ground is healed
Gaining momentum
Steadily welcoming creation
With all its beauty blossoming
The river of substance
No more concealed.

Untroubled by time's
        self-made space
Formal courtships
        now commencing
As waters dance
With sun-tipped allies
Flickering amidst
        Its opiate grace.

Follow

Follow your heart
Not your head
- That's what he said -
            And I believed him.
For my heart showed me
How to chart new journeys
      How to explore devastated rivers
That carried years of guilt
And how to show compassion
When what I really felt
                  Was rage.
He told me it was just
        A test
To wake every morning
And invest in me
        So that I could help others
Lost in their own company
And my unfaltering chest
Wholeheartedly agreed.
As I listened to the tempo
      The movement
            The cadency
My heart told me
      To rise when I sat
            In my fickled head
Talking myself out of adventure
And back into a bed that
Longed to keep me
      Captivated
            Frustrated
                  And empty.

But the beat
    The temptation
The honest rhythm
         And sensation
That shook me awake
Made me burst with delirious
Sparks that life lent me
        To share in my own way
    To give for my own sake
        My own sanity!

Follow your heart
Not your head
- That's what I said -
      And she believed me.
For your heart will show you
     Your path
Unweed your knotted dreams
And ask you to believe
Things your head
      Would have you wipe clean.

Your Affliction

Should I care that the light from inside
Has dulled since I last felt you feel alive?
Should I cry for a heart that twists and
Runs away, towards plans that sit in another's dream?
Should I pity the indecisive mind that rages with
Intelligence, but is ignorant to itself?
Should I laugh at the simplicity of it all and
Give you the answer you already have?
Would you like me to?

Would you run a million lives away to escape the
Truth I like to call my sanctuary?
Would you stop your soul from listening and cover
Ears with hands once used to rock your babes to sleep?
Could I make you see the worth in the tiny actions
That can build a whole?
Would you like me to?

If I stole a thousand wishes, could you choose
The one that sells a piece of peace to you?
If I let you take the pen, could you write the
Promise that allows life in through you?
Should I tell you that you're loved and love will
Swallow oceans full of greed until it's time to go?
Would you like me to?
  Do you want me to?
    Would you believe me?

10th June 2016 - 3.33am

I watch your face
as you listen to me explain
      confused
              drained
it tells me that you
don't understand
or even pretend to know
how this version of us
       got so out of hand.
But the space that exists between
my anguish and your silence
is where our love lives
and forgives the differences
between our sexes.

30th May 2016 - 11.48pm

There is a moment
a single fragment of time
- one exact point -
when the dream you have cradled
   kept safe and worked for
            longed for
                  your entire life for
terminally fades with silent applause.
The moment comes and goes
slowly then quickly
and you are never the same again.
Nothing shines as brightly
your world
         your universe
- makes no sense -
When the moment is gone
will you even remember it?
If someone asked
when was it your dream passed?
Would you know?
Or would you say: 'about 47'.
About 47?
Not the precise day, hour, second?
Not the very instant your dream
beckoned another to come inside
and close the door?
You have to ask: was it ever your dream at all?
Or were you just holding it?
Waiting for someone else to become
strong enough to lift it
   bold enough to risk it
      brave enough to call it their own.

Lie Down

Sometimes the weight is too much.
            Do you feel it?
     How long can you hold you up?
Pictures of the past
Flood your eyes so it's all
           You can see
   - Smothering you -
   Drenching your sight
And you wonder if you'll ever
                See properly again.
Ears pulse from fruitless crying
            But the tears don't help
                They just fall
And lying painfully in your lap
            They sigh
Waiting to be brushed away
Waiting to be mopped up
            And thrown into another day.

Lie down.

            Remember how
The years have passed
            And nothing much has changed
Apart from the truth
            That just as years pass
So have the people that once claimed
To know you
            Love you
                Hate you.

Lie down.

Remember how
What you once wrote
                Remains pitifully the same
The doubts
    The questions
The ones with no answers
            And no-one to give chances
                Away for free
Or keep your place in the cue for emotional debris.

Lie down.

        Remember how
You've done this a thousand times
            Bribed your way out of a solution
            Sold to the highest bidder.
                    Consider this moment
            The one that sits beside you
                Holding your angry dreams
And how you know it's the last time
            You want to remember.
The last time you milk your eyes
                For the sake of a journey
            Filled with lies
And destroyed by the time it takes to
        Sit up!
            Stand up!
                    Times up!

Cycle of Life

She glided from one to another
        Absorbed
Hypnotised by a thousand yellow fruits
Inquisitively searching
Filling herself with the
        Essence of summer
Intoxicated with the delights
Mother Nature had provided
Humming a song that she alone
Had been taught to recognise
        As her own.

She sang
Knowing the translation would erupt
Into a mass of sticky riches
With gold and amber velvet streams
- Enticing -
Never tiring
Relentlessly enquiring
As the cycle of life
Took pleasure in her company.

I watched her lift
Her swollen body
Allowing the warm air to
Mould itself around her form
Transporting her
Towards the ecstatic sun.
A sting shattered
And my jealous chest caved
As my hand raised
To catch the pain from falling.
Her world
Her life
Though shorter and less apparent
Seemed more vital
In that moment
Than mine.

2nd July 2016 - 12.45am

You didn't want me to exist.
Would you rather I left?
Or fade into the kitchen and
hide behind the smiles and
wine bottles that live there
      - orphaned -
            silenced.
Do I remind you of someone
who fills your heart with fear?
Does my presence make your gut tense?
Or is it who I represent?
  Tell me
      - confess -
so you don't make a mess
                  when I leave.

20th April 2017 - 12.07pm

My bow and arrow
fits inside my handbag.
The strength to use it
sits inside my heart.

Let Go

Touch her hand
It's ok, she's not cold yet
A shade from pale
But still here
Holding on to let you hold on to her
Blending into the pillow's lace
She opens her eyes to see your pain
And offers a smile
Her last?
Bodies close in around you
Your shoulders collapse
Folding in on themselves
The weight too much to bear
But not enough to yet surrender.
She reaches out to comfort you
To stroke your tense arm
Will she feel it?
The terror
The unholy desperate need to run
Will you be the last thing she feels?
Will you ever forget how she felt?
Her waxy flesh
Her tiny, claw-like fingers
Telling you it's nearly time
To leave the burdens and the struggle behind.
The relentless fever of life spikes
Burning
Sweat covered and deliriously confusing.

'It's ok,' you say, 'let go.'
She nods.
Her breath rattles
Her chest light
She pulls a little
She needs you near
Her voice travels
On a different current
And floats to a place inside.
'It's ok,' she says, 'let go.'

19th February 2016 - 4.01am

Love stops being a feeling
  something to tell your
    friends about
      boast about
        joke about
when the darkest hour of
your life knocks at the door
and he answers it for you.

23rd January 2017 - 11.02pm

To share your pain with my body
was all that I could give.
Introductions weren't necessary
we'd already met.

Don't Stay in Dreams (a whisper to a son)

I could fill your humbled ruined dreams
With all the things
   I've done and seen.
     Tell you to fight
       When you feel like flying
Leave the night
  When it finds you
Lying and rising to its game.
Don't take the bate
The hate will be enough
To destroy your every thought
And every waking moment
  Will torment you
Until you're bought and sold
Back to the night
   - Back to the lies -
Throw open your windows
      Rise
The morning light will feed you
  If you ask it to.

Don't stay in dreams too long, dear.
Fanciful desires hold hands
With forgotten fears.
  Stay wide awake
    Both eyes open
Make your way in the sunshine
And dine under a ruby tree.
Walk your path

Passionately
Take your mission
Seriously
Catastrophes are there
To be smiled at
For they will light the road you roam
- With lessons learned -
Grown out of courage.

Should-have-beens and Halos

Wholly insignificant
- Controlled by people -
    I don't know.
Talked over by those
    Who don't listen.
Sold out by people who
    Don't buy into me.
Who told them that they counted
For more than I could
Ever have amounted to?
Who drew up my plan
And left no instructions
    For some kind of elaborate rescue?
Tip-toeing around a garden full
Of duty and consideration
Whilst my back yard is filled
With accusation and
The rotting remains of
Should-have-beens and halos.

But I'm no saint
    And I'm no victim.
        Untie my hands
Take your politics from out of my mouth
And let me speak
        My truth.

29th April 2017 - 2.32am

I have no food
    for your love.
      It is too greedy
  too savage
and too hollow.
    There's no banquet
      under my command
    that could
      fill you up!

3rd February 2017 - 2.49am

As I step on your chalk words and
wait for the rain to wash them away
I watch the colour drain from
- your promises and hopes -
choked by deliberate falsehoods
cloaked with exuberant gestures
dreams that never once belonged
                              to you.
They came from my palette.
They came from my heart.

4th September 2017 – 2.24am

Shine in the low
where the dirt
and the worst
part of you knows
it can't escape.
 - Shine -
and don't
let it take
you with it.

Look Deeper

What is it you're looking for
In my face?
The indignation of a lifetime
That has been exhausted
By problems that
Have no solutions?
Or are you looking
To exonerate
Yourself from a blame
You think you should
Be carrying?

24th December 2016 - 1.57am

Every inch of my being
has been coloured in
with your pen.
  All but one.
In that singular inch
 - lies my soul -
and that is my canvas
to paint or to taint
any way that I wish.

29th November 2016 - 4.26am

When the final touch has been touched
        and the final kiss kissed
    when the lights go out
and you lie there
    in your own world
        with your own thoughts
            - your own visions -
who do you pretend to be?
Is that the real view?
The *you* your soul's allowing you to see
just for a minute or two
presenting honesty
        and the many routes
            you could take
the many trails you could explore.
        And I wonder
            could the other
23 hours and 58 minutes
        just be bullshit
            - wasting time and settling scores -
    unless at least
        some of it is spent
            crossing paths.

Sit with my heart a while
and I will share with you
the beat of my life.

Join the author on Instagram: @f.a.peeke

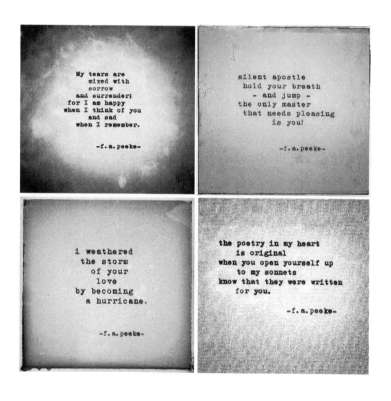

My tears are
mixed with
sorrow
and surrender;
for I am happy
when I think of you
and sad
when I remember.

-f.a.peeke-

silent apostle
hold your breath
- and jump -
the only master
that needs pleasing
is you!

-f.a.peeke-

i weathered
the storm
of your
love
by becoming
a hurricane.

-f.a.peeke-

the poetry in my heart
is original
when you open yourself up
to my sonnets
know that they were written
for you.

-f.a.peeke-

Or visit: www.fapeeke.com